UP AND DOWN
THE TOTEM POLE

UP AND DOWN THE TOTEM POLE

AN ACCOUNT OF ADULT MENTAL HEALTH AND DRUG ABUSE

ROSEMARIE BOOLER

Matador
9 Priory Business Park
Kibworth Beauchamp
Leicestershire LE8 0RX, UK
Tel: (+44) 116 279 2299
Fax: (+44) 116 279 2277
Email: books@troubador.co.uk
Web: www.troubador.co.uk/matador

ISBN 978 1784622 008

British Library Cataloguing in Publication Data.
A catalogue record for this book is available from the British Library.

Printed and bound in the UK by TJ International, Padstow, Cornwall
Typeset in Aldine by Troubador Publishing Ltd

Matador is an imprint of Troubador Publishing Ltd

Dedicated to my darling daughter Danielle, my perfect baby, beautiful child and adored young lady. You light up my soul, a true gift from God.

And Mr S. Smith for kissing me awake!!!

CONTENTS

Chapter 1

HEROIN WHORE

I love you more than my partner, more than my children, more than life. I lie to myself, I steal from everyone I can, I deceive. I am cheating, I am in love with you my little brown soother, I want more of you each passing day, I can't get enough of you, I inhale as much of you as fast as I can.

Once I had friends, parents, partners and children I loved...now they are in the way of my brown lover. I spend seven years out of every ten waiting for you in the pouring rain, I give all of my mind, body and soul to you, all my money and everything I own and value goes to you. I snatch ten minutes from work, home, then you still want more of me, you want all of me.

At first you made me itch and be sick but I didn't care, you eased my mind, anaesthetised my brain and body, we felt relaxed together, no longer anxious and on a come down, now just mellow and all for just a tenner.

You are supposed to be my bit on the side... now you are blackmailing me you conniving bitch. I do everything for you, I work, run the car, skip food and still you want more from me... you and your circle of friends, what do you call them, Whites, E's, Speed, Dexis you plead innocence, a cheap ride back down in comfort, no shakes no anxiety.

You are so nice, so seductive, great fun with my smack head mates, we do have a laugh, you feel so nice inside of me. I just want more and more of you, to just spend time with you over the weekend, treat myself to your lovely presence after a hard week at work.

I work for you, I am a devoted loyal slave of yours, I'll do anything you ask of me. I'll rob from the old ladies, their pension will last for a whole day with you, I want all of my friends to get to know you, safety in numbers, besides when they are all chasing you they pay for my habit.

No longer am I Mr. nice guy, now you have come to live in my body I have thrown out everything decent about me, you control everything, it's easier for me, good excuse, loads of sympathy from do gooders.

People are scared of you, I am not, you look just like dust and vanish into a little black beetle and then a whiff of smoke. You taste disgusting and smell even worse but I don't care about your appearance. Come to think about it I don't care about mine either, I don't care about the mess the house is in, you don't mind, you are at home in the filth being the dirty whore you are. My partner hates you, is jealous and knows I am cheating on them to be with you. Job gone, opp's got caught skiving good and proper, never mind, got three of my colleagues on our side.

I wanted to escape my mind and you helped me to do this, I am a changed man, no longer the young ambitious good looking dude, clean shaven, ironed clothes, career, car, in love with the leggy blond who caught my eye by the photocopier. I, instead, have gone for the rugged look, you know, dirty, ripped jeans, stubble, no longer down the gym admiring my six pack.

Now skinny and pale and even though only five years have passed I have aged twenty, but not in wisdom and knowledge just physically. No car no more, unless I steal someone else's and drive drugged up with no insurance. No job no more, no income, partner's left me and took the kids… I hadn't noticed things had got that bad. Now homeless, no choice must now lead a life of crime to support you my little brown whore. I think I am paranoid, I think the police are watching me come and go from my house and are watching who else are coming round.

I live on a respectable street even though I am not respectable. Oh, good news, I'm not paranoid the police are watching me, they are not as stupid as we think and they look.

I have an addictive personality, I am a heroin addict come to think of it. I am addicted to everything addict able, chocolate, coffee, cigarettes, dope, green, alcohol, crack cocaine, heroin… the things on this list that are legal still kill you.

Can you remember the first drag of a fag you had, thirteen years old was my first time, a shared packet of ten consulate menthol. We were hiding down Ghost Lane and just puffing, we didn't even know how to hold it and it tasted disgusting, not to worry we kept on trying, spluttering and choking. Then one hot summer's day at Foxton Locks I had my first B & H, my friend warned me not to inhale it so of course I did... BANG... total head rush feeling giddy and sick my head pounding... And bingo another in on the towpath! Since then all my spare money over the last thirty years has gone on supporting one addiction after another.

'Wow' that first hit, of everything you remember, then chase that first high, but no one gets you quite there, so you do more and more and still not get the high of the first time. The easiest way to stop expensive bad habits is not to start (try) them in the first place. They are for losers and if you are successful you will soon turn into a loser. Once an addict always an addict, just trying not to indulge in whatever your bag is.

Alcohol is a depressant, it gives you a dose of bi-polar (manic depression) first it loosens your inhibitions, it is legal cheap and available 24/7 and you don't notice yourself slipping gently into it. It kills over 40,000 people per year in this country alone.

Heading a life of crime and grime, passed caring, more illegal, more daring.

Chapter 2

FELT TIP PINK RABBITS

My dad had started building the bungalow at Foxton, the doctors had said that my mum would be in a wheelchair before Christmas so time was of the essence. My parents had taken out a bridging loan to raise enough money to do it before Christmas. Our three bed detached house in Harborough was on the market and the country was in recession so houses were hard to sell.

My sister having just learned to draw rabbits had gone into every room and decorated every white glossed windowsill with them. Mum had tried to wash them off but to no avail, my dad came home and went mad, the only way to get rid of them was to sand the window ledges down, undercoat and repaint them. He was furious and being already under financial stress and the added stress of mum's illness, he just flipped demanding to know which one of us had done the dirty deed, my sister denied it being too terrified of the consequences. I was telling the truth when I said I hadn't done it and if my dad had stopped to think two minutes he would have known that A: *I couldn't draw that well* and B: *I wasn't tall enough to reach the windowsills anyway.* He just saw red, he was sitting on the sofa as I stood in front of him, he had hold of me by my left arm as he kept smacking my right leg. He was smacking me so hard it was knocking me over bar his grip on my left arm I would have gone flying. He kept repeating himself for me to 'tell the truth' and to say 'I had done it' I was telling the truth it wasn't me, and my sister was too scared by now to admit it. Eventually I was sent to my room sobbing so hard I could hardly breath. When my dad had calmed down my sister admitted to him that it was her. His venom had all been spent on me so she was just sent to her room. Dad knocked on my door, opened it far enough to stick his head round and muttered that he was sorry, I couldn't speak so I just nodded my head and he closed the door. I never forgave him, to this day I have never forgave nor forgotten this incident. Alongside the smacks both my parents gave me, they taught me not to trust anyone or love them either.

I was a difficult child as it was and this escalated me into a fearless, reckless and delinquent child. I know my parents were not trying to kill me and when I was smacked I just bit my lip and said, 'that didn't hurt,' which just exasperated them.

Chapter 3

CONSULATE DOWN GHOST LANE

It's always dark down here, dark and damp. Ghost Lane runs from Middle Street to Swingbridge Street behind the vicarage and behind the rec. It's where all wanna be smokers come for their first few tentative drags.

I had just started the morning village paper round for the shop that Mr. and Mrs Braughton ran, the few pounds bought my Menthol consulate ten pack. Nowadays a shopkeeper knowing that you are just thirteen years old would not sell you fags, yet Mr. and Mrs Braughton had no reserves over this, just more money in the till for them. So, there we were me and my mate Sophie, armed with ten fags, a box of swan matches and extreme excitement and anxiety over being caught.

I should have had an idyllic childhood brought up in a picture postcard village with a population of 500 people. The village was mainly made up of three interrelated families mixed with the posh privileged families in the big houses. We moved to Foxton when I was nine years old. My dad's a builder and my mum had multiple sclerosis so he built her a bungalow of her design before she became too ill to climb the stairs. My dad was mardy most of the time and we never know what mood my mum would be in when we got home from school.

I wasn't diagnosed with manic depression until I was twenty seven when I walked down the street naked believing with my whole heart that I was bringing on the rapture 'a Christian philosophy' that Jesus would return and take all the loyal fellowmen to heaven before the tribulation and Armageddon. How vain, to think I was perfect and responsible to save all humanity. Anyway I am jumping the Gun.

My first puff of a cigarette was when I was six years old, I was blackmailing the babysitters saying I would tell my parents they had been smoking unless they let me try it. One spluttering drag and I was hooked, I couldn't wait until I was big enough to start smoking.

Chapter 4

WHERE I'M AT

I was always looking for escape from reality and my troubled mind, I didn't know what was wrong with me, I just knew I was different. I was suffering from chronic anxiety and depression but I hadn't heard of either of them and children were not diagnosed anyway.

Anything addictable I take, smoking, drinking, coffee, chocolate, speed, ecstasy, ketamin, which is a tranquilliser for horses, cocaine, crack cocaine and heroin, anything to get off my head and allow me to day dream away from reality. Even if my life was perfect, enough money, nice, loving, good relationship with my daughter and partner I would screw things up. My mood is all over the place. I don't know from one day to the next how I am going to feel. My partner says it's like having ten girlfriends in one body.

Just finished smoking the last few lines of smack (heroin) I console myself with the fact that at least I don't jack up (inject it).

My daughter came round this morning proudly showing me the tacky tattoo she has had done. I hate tattoos and she's been fool enough to have the date she started seeing her boyfriend, I didn't pass comment, I hate arguing with her and I am a fine one to talk. I have never had a tattoo I don't like them.

Writing this book is harder than I imagined, I thought it would just flow out of me and I could just write the way I think. I can't write it down fast enough to keep up with my thoughts.

Let's try starting somewhere other than where I'm at…

Chapter 5

MEMORIES... PAST

I lost my virginity when I was thirteen, I was a late developer physically and my nipples had just budded and I hardly had any pubic hair. When my boyfriend slipped his hand in my knickers he said, 'you've got no pubes.' I was way too young physically, emotionally and mentally. I thought by having sex with him would keep him interested.

My dad caught us in my bedroom when they got in, we lived in a bungalow and my boyfriend would climb out of the window. My parents hated him, called him a water gypsy because he lived on a boat. My mum said to me, 'when you grow up you'll be a horse.' I didn't know what losing your virginity had got to do with horses. I asked loads of people what she meant and they explained, not 'a horse a whore.'

They threw me out when I was fourteen and I went to live with my Auntie. My mum wanted to put me in a children's home but my Auntie took me in. I was a brilliant actress and could act as though butter wouldn't melt in my mouth, underneath my façade I was a conniving, spiteful bitch that was full of jealousy and bitterness.

All children try to please their parents to win their love and acceptance, I did try half-heartedly but my parents couldn't cope with a manic-depressive child. It's hard work, it's hard work for my friends and my boyfriend. My mood swings from one extreme to the other, the bubbly confident extrovert flips into anxiety followed by self-loathing and severe depression. In the last fifteen years if you add all the times I have spent in hospital on a mental ward it amounts to six years.

Present: I am sweating buckets as I write this, projectile vomiting in the kitchen sink, I haven't eaten so it's just coffee puke induced by smack fags and coffee on an empty stomach.

Back to the mental ward: There is a mixture of different patients from schizophrenics, depressives, manic-depressives, alcoholics and drug addicts. The staff are so busy with paperwork they don't have the time to talk, there is no counselling other than that the patients give to each other. Listening to the life histories of the other patients gets your own problems into perspective.

I was never sexually abused as a child, physically, emotionally and mentally but never sexually. I have a sister who is thirteen months older than me and she was so frightened of being smacked that she was the 'perfect' child, I was the rebel. She's a spiteful bitch that would grass me up over everything I did wrong and be smirking while I was being smacked.

I punched my mum in the face when I was fourteen, I had had enough of being smacked by her, she couldn't walk without an A frame. I sent her flying across the hall into the desk and knocked her out, I just picked up my school bag and cookery basket (had cooking lesson at school that day) and just went and caught the bus, this was the reason I went to live at my Aunties.

My mind jumps from one idea to another so please excuse the lack of consistency in this writing. I confessed to my boyfriend earlier this week that I had been unfaithful. I hate infidelity yet I had done it, there is no excuse for it even though at the time I had drank a bottle of sambucca and smoked two bags of smack, I was off my head. My boyfriend is the best thing that happened in my life bar having my daughter and I was unfaithful, what a slut. Even worse is that he said I should have taken it to the grave with me but my weak guilty mind couldn't keep the truth from him, I had to tell him, I couldn't live with it on my conscience. Worse still, I gave him venereal warts, my ex husband gave them to me, I didn't get them but now my boyfriend has them and they are a permanent reminder of my disgusting unfaithful mess. He didn't deserve it, he is the most perfect gentleman and I trust him totally, he didn't even shout or lose his temper, he just loves me so much and I love him. We are complete opposites, he is calm, loyal and stable, nothing rocks his boat. I am flighty, messy and all over the place. He gets up in the morning and does an honest days work as a self-employed carpenter and plasterer. Because we are in a recession he hasn't got much work on, yet he still gets up, cuts wood up for the fire and works on his and his dad's allotment. He's told his sister that I was unfaithful and she will tell his parents, my name will be mud, more than it is already.

Chapter 6

SUICIDE SURVIVOR

Just waiting for smack to be delivered, got a new supplier that will bring it to my house. This means I don't have to get dressed and go out to score. Safer this way, less chance of being caught.

For someone who is a walking bad habit, I believe in God. I believe I will go to heaven and that all the bad things I have done will be forgiven, I read a lot of self-help books on spirituality.

I have tried to commit suicide three times. The first was when I was twelve, I took slug pellets, this was to get my sister in trouble with my parents. They had left her in charge whilst they were out getting treatment for my mum's MS, all it did was made me feel violently sick and gave me an upset stomach and a sore throat from throwing up bracken. The second two attempts were much later on. When I was thirty-eight I took two months worth of sleeping tablets then chickened out, I called my friend and was taken to hospital to be wired up to loads of machines. When I had slept it off I was discharged from hospital and had to get a taxi back from Leicester to Market Harborough. It cost twenty pounds,

I thought I would be taken to the mental ward but I was just taken home and dropped off.

The last time I tried I really meant business. I took months worth of medication, I had saved up for the event 'sleepers' 'tranquillisers' 'mood stabilisers' 'anti-depressants' I took the lot. I had a friend staying with me at the time and he forgot to lock the front door when he went out to work in the morning, then by chance another friend called round. I had been unconscious for seventeen hours and had inhaled my vomit and wet the bed. I was in intensive care for five days and then in hospital for five months afterwards, I meant it to end my life. By the grace of God and my two friend's coincidental action I am still here. There must be a reason I survived.

Twenty per cent that's one in five manic-depressives commit suicide that's a lot. It just shows how hard this illness is to live with, we all have the same tendencies to throw our lives up in the air when we are high, spend money we haven't got, be promiscuous. Being high is great fun, loads of energy... fast living and laughing, then comes the down, what goes up must come down, and crashing down is what happens.

I take as much medication enough to send an elephant to sleep, the doctors prefer you depressed, you are easier to look after. When you are depressed you are less trouble and safer than when you are high.

Chapter 7

CAREERS AND PARENTHOOD

For years my friends have told me to write a book, they say my life is like a soap opera, people coming and going.

I used to have a house full when my daughter lived with me. To make ends meet I did some child minding, packed fabric, worked behind bars and in a nightclub. Money was always tight but I was happy.

I adore my child and have always put her interests first, she was my wake up call, it was time to grow up. I had always earned a good wage before I had my daughter, I sold computers by day and worked behind bars in the evening. Being manic gave me enough energy to hold down two full time jobs and I just kept going. I was never short of a boyfriend, I was slim, made up to the nines and a bundle of fun and games.

When I met my ex husband I was looking for someone who would be a good father, he was a crap husband, brilliant father. My daughter lived with me until she was six, disaster struck, my boyfriend at the time was involved in an industrial accident whilst working, he died tragically.

A friend of mine of fifteen years died of a septic leg from years of injecting heroin, then on 21st May the same year, my mum died three close deaths in one month. Then my ex husband seized the moment took my child from me allowing me to see her just one hour per week under the supervision of her nana, I was devastated.

My life had gone from 24/7 busy hectic and fun to complete grief and misery. No one came round, no one knew what to say to me, what was there to say? My busy, noisy house with lots of children, friends, work and boyfriend had gone into total silence. I wasn't capable of working, the grief and depression took a grip on me that even twelve years later cuts like a knife.

Chapter 8

BOYFRIEND AND A BUNDLE OF FUN

My boyfriend has literally saved my life and made me feel like living again. I still don't get dressed unless I have to go out, which is rare. I just go into town to pay my bills once a month otherwise I stay in my dressing gown, not washing or brushing my teeth. I don't keep the house clean any more, my boyfriend does everything for me and my friend pops down the corner shop for milk and coffee.

I wasn't expecting my life to turn out like this. You never know what life is going to throw at you. You just have to keep going hoping and praying that things will get better. I don't work, I haven't worked since my boyfriend died. I live at £6000 below the official bread line. I didn't know what poverty was until I split up with my ex husband.

My parents were wealthy and I was always employable as I was a bundle of fun, extrovert and had boundless energy. In bars people would say, 'I'll have half a pint of whatever she's on' or they would say to me 'keep taking the tablets.' I thought, 'what tablets' little did I know, that's the thing with mental illness everyone else can see it but yourself. I used to think what's wrong with everyone else, why are they so depressed? I wasn't aware it was me that was as high as a kite. I could drink like a fish, I was always drunk and disorderly or smoking weed, taking speed, being full of excitement, laughs and then the big despair and black depression. My nightmares were so vivid that from the first few moments of waking I would still be in the horror of the nightmare.

Chapter 9

TRAIN TRACK TRAUMA

When I was seventeen waiting for the train to take me to college in Leicester I saw a man commit suicide, he was dressed smartly and carrying a briefcase and looked just like any other business man off to work for the day. It was January and really cold, the man walked down the steps on the opposite side of the station, the side going to Kettering. He just laid on the track, there was nothing anyone could do as the train came in and chopped his head off. Afterwards you could have heard a pin drop, besides the shock of it, it sent me hysterical but not crying hysterical... laughing, I just kept saying did you see that he's just had his head chopped off. One of the other commuters told me she would slap me if I didn't stop laughing, I went into the ladies and lay on the floor crippled with laughter and tears at the same time. My friend who was doing the same hairdressing course couldn't stop shaking and crying, me, thinking I was grown up, helped her on to the train that was now an hour late due to the commotion. We arrived at college only to be told to go home as we were both in shock, all I kept thinking was ignorant bastard, why commit suicide in front of all the children travelling to school. I considered at the ripe old age of seventeen that I was a fully grown adult and thought he should have done it further down the track where no one could see it. Seconds after he had done it I thought I could see him staring in shocked wonder at his corpse, then he looked directly into my eyes and vanished like a mirage.

This was only the beginning; my boyfriend at the time, his father was the ambulance driver that had to stitch the head back on to the body for the deceased relative to identify him.

I worked part time at the hairdressers that his wife used and when they rang her to come and identify him she said she would be there after she had had her hair done, talk about priorities. Because of these coincides I felt linked to the dead man. I kept having nightmares about it, the nightmares were so vivid I could still see him mocking me with his headless corpse holding his briefcase in one hand and his severed head in the other when I woke up.

In those days there was no counselling for people who had had a traumatic experience, I couldn't talk to anyone about it, this was my first of many brushes with suicide.

Chapter 10

COCKTAILS ON THE WARD

One of my closest friends took sixteen paracetamol and a half bottle of brandy, she telephoned her boyfriend to tell him what she had done. He thought she was calling his bluff and just wanted him to come home from the pub there and then. He ignored her call and turned up at the house at closing time being too late to save her, it took four days of excruciating pain for her to die.

Paracetamol rots your internal organs and slowly your body just packs up, you start to poo out your liver.

She left a seven-year-old daughter. Four days she knew she was going to die and nothing could save her, she didn't want to die and lived through hell until she did. No one could understand it she was beautiful, had a gorgeous daughter, a nice house, boyfriend and lots of friends, it was all such a shock no one was expecting it.

Sometimes a cry for help goes unheard with disastrous consequences. Nine out of every ten suicides are cries for help, very few people want to end their lives abruptly. They must can't deal with what life is throwing at them at the time and committing suicide seems the only option, there is a lot of bottled up anger and resentment towards the people you love and you don't feel they love you.

A dear friend of mine, who died recently of a brain tumour, tried suicide on the ward. She was being specialised left with one nurse to her self because of the risk of her harming herself. She went to the toilet and her nurse was standing outside chatting to the other staff about her holiday photos. She wasn't paying attention to how long my friend was in the toilet. Eventually the nurse realised and opened the door from the outside to find her hanging from a shoelace tied around the sink. I was on the ward telephone at the time and saw everything. The crash team arrived and they jump-started her heart. She was in intensive care and then brought back to the ward, you could see the bruising and the deep strangle lines around her throat. She survived but things like this shouldn't happen on a mental ward, you are supposed to be safe in there, it just goes to show you're not... the staff are supposedly there to help you, but they're not. They just get paid a fortune for their presence.

I was in the smoke room on the ward when another patient, who again had a nurse with him 24/7, threw himself through the plate glass window from the 1st floor, he survived a lot of broken bones but he lived.

Some of the things that go on in mental wards are beyond belief, we have less worth than chickens on a battery farm.

Chapter 11

THE BEST CHOCOLATE ICE CREAM

Two women I knew who were manic-depressives committed suicide in the same week. I don't know how they did it I just read it in the local papers hatch, match, dispatch (obituaries.)

A lot of us have dual – diagnosis mental health problems coupled with alcohol or drug abuse, I do all three, anything to escape the deep depression and mad highs. I get all sorts of grandeur ideas in my head. I think I can save the world. It is disgusting what happens on the planet, we all need our heads banging together.

My dad used to do that to me and my sister 'bang our heads together' when we were naughty. It had more to do with him stressed out from work and from our mother.

My sister would say we had a privileged upbringing but I don't see it like that. Although there was no shortage of money and we lived in a big bungalow there was no love or affection. I don't have one happy memory of my father, and very few of my mother. When my mum was in a good mood… when, she was a good laugh. Although she was in a wheelchair she had a good sense of humour when she wasn't being bitter and twisted.

I remember one occasion before Christmas, both my sister and I had left home and dad had told mum she could have just one tin of Quality Street over Christmas. My mum telephoned me to ask me to take her to Woolco at Oadby to get more chocolates. I couldn't get her wheelchair put together and we were both in hysterics, every time I asked a passing man to help he thought it was some kind of candid camera prank and wouldn't help. When eventually we got my mum into her wheelchair she bought every type of boxed chocolates they had for sale, she had the basket on her knees and was loaded down to the max with chocolates. We then went to Bejams and bought every flavour of ice cream that they sold. I had not got the strength to push her up the sloping ramp to the car park, eventually a staff member came to our assistance, this day is one of my happiest memories of my mum. It was pure good fun until I got her home and dad turned up, he blamed me for all the chocolates and said I shouldn't have taken her. I didn't care, we had had such a fun day together, I will remember it always.

Chapter 12

SEVENTIES SHORTS

Skipping subjects, I've no idea how to get this writing into chapter's and follow the same thought track, I am grateful as a friend has offered to type and edit my content, I am confident she will sort it out for me.

Sitting here with my boyfriend Steve and best friend Sarah the conversation is about another friend who we think is a paedophile. I'm drunk and smoking smack listening to the radio. Talking about the paedophile makes my skin crawl, Sarah met him at the resource centre (a place for the mentally ill to congregate) and he is always inappropriately dressed. He wears a woman's T-shirt style night dress and seventies running shorts, you know, the ones 'with the net lining' he sits with his legs open so you can see his balls through the net. I banned him from coming round to my house unless he had jogging bottoms on. It was embarrassing to look at him but he seemed to like making his audience feel uncomfortable, I think it gave him some sort of perverse pleasure to make people uncomfortable around him.

At one point when I was trying to sell my house I had my possessions stored in his garage, Steve and I went over to collect stuff and were invited into his flat. Mike isn't diagnosed with any illness but is obviously not normal, whatever that is. His flat is totally full of old newspapers, McDonald's cartons and any crap you can think of. There is nowhere to sit and is the sort of place you would not accept a cup of coffee or tea, I don't think he has thrown away anything in the fifteen years he has lived there.

At the time Steve and I called he had a female friend there, Janice, who was colouring in a children's colouring book and proudly showed Steve and I her work, she was good at not going over the lines for a thirty year old. It was obvious that Janice had learning difficulties and when she started showing us the photo's it became more apparent. 'These are my budgies' she proudly said, showing us a photo of a cage containing one live budgie and one dead one on the floor of the cage. She then started going on about moving in with her boyfriend and gave us details of how he had asked her to send photo's of herself in naughty waitress outfits etc., she then pulled out a photo of Ryan Gigg the footballer. It was one of those situations when… you wanted to laugh out loud but had to turn your head because you couldn't hide the smile creeping on to your face.

Another friend of mine is bisexual and suffers from OCD (*obsessive compulsive disorder*) her advanced housing flat is immaculate, she spends four days cleaning her bathroom and at one point wouldn't let anyone in and slept at a friend's flat in the same building. She was having a lesbian affair with Star one of the paedophile's friends, because Andy was driving Star over to Tina's house they felt obliged to let Andy watch them. While they were getting on with what lesbians do Andy was squirting lemon jiff kitchen cleaner mousse down his japs eye, no wonder he can't get an erection anymore. The things people do never cease to amaze me.

Chapter 13

FUCKED UP FRIENDS

Another friend of mine is an alcoholic trying not to drink eight cans of strong cider a day and was invited to spend the night at a party Star was having, the party members being herself, Tina, Star and Mike. Mike had bought enough alcohol to sink a ship and my friend got overly pissed and fell down the stairs, they left her there on the sofa to sleep it off, not one of them having the sense to take her to A & E. In the morning my friend went to hospital and all Star was bothered about was that my friend had broken her Hoover when she fell down the stairs. Fair-weather friends don't care if you near enough die in front of them, as long as they can carry on drinking and performing whatever perversity they are into. Tina is now going out with a friend of mine, she has given up her lesbian activity for the time being and is totally in love with Gary.

Gary has been stabbed seven times and his brother once bit his finger so badly it is now deformed. Gary's brother committed suicide about four months ago and Gary insists it has changed him from the drug abusive alcoholic he is. Gary is totally oblivious to how he is and what he's about. He is a violent bully and thinks he is a good catch for any woman. He is using Tina for all she is worth. Tina is overweight and very bubbly, in fact she has a lovely personality albeit very gullible and naïve. Gary will con anyone and everyone to pay for his alcohol and drugs. Tina knows about his drinking but not the heroin. Gary just tips half a bottle of brandy down his throat but claims he doesn't like alcohol! He suddenly went blind (partially) overnight and puts it down to stress, I'm more inclined to think it has something to do with drug abuse. He once was a chef and was studying psychology, he has yet to wake up and realise that life will never be the same for him, he is now one of us, unemployable, he was a waster anyway. He thinks he's a good parent to his four-year-old daughter yet he is a total control freak. His mother found his brother dead from an overdose of alcohol substitute medication. He was dead lying in a pool of his own piss and excrement. He had tried to rape his mother and sister the month before his suicide and Gary had knocked him out over it, not surprising.

All of my friends have colourful lives, no one I know is what you might call normal, you know, just regular people going to work, married and supporting a family and watching TV soap operas in the evening. Steve and I are so poor we can't afford a TV set let alone the license fee. We just listen to the radio and talk.

This book is supposed to tell my story about going from menthol cigarettes to being a full blown heroin addict, but I keep getting side tracked and talking about the people I know who are just as fucked up as I am.

Chapter 14

OH SO LONELY

When my friend died (who had once been my boyfriend) another friend died at the same time, then my mum died shortly after, and my daughter went to live with her dad, I was so lonely. My house went from being full of children, friends and neighbours I was devastated.

I went from being busy 24/7 hectic but happy, not enough hours in the day to accomplish all that needed to doing, to nothing, no boyfriend, friend, my daughter gone and no one coming round. I was so lonely, desolate and the house was silent, the only visitor was my support worker who told me time would heal me. It hasn't, and still miss my loved ones just as much. Time lets you accept what has happened and you learn to live with it.

My daughter is now eighteen and drop dead gorgeous, full of life and energy, she takes pride in her appearance. She is always made up and dressed fashionably showing off her ample breasts with low cut tops. She is sitting her A levels at the moment and hopes to go to university in Sheffield. From the time when she was when I only saw her for one hour a week has gone by quickly in a haze of chopped up loneliness, I wanted company and any company would do, better than being alone with my depression and grief. I didn't bother eating, washing or brushing my teeth. I was in and out of hospital like a revolving door. I preferred being in hospital at least I had company. I sat in the smoking room all night talking to whoever else was up with their confused madness and insomnia.

I have lost a lot of friends through suicide and sheer quantities of prescribed medication. We all die younger than most people, that's a silly thing to say, one in five people with my diagnosis bi-polar as it is called now commit suicide. It just goes to show how hard this is to live with, I can't imagine what my life would be like if I didn't have it.

Chapter 15

DEALERSHIP

I need to go down to the corner shop, I need coffee and another disposable lighter. I'll get twenty pounds cash back on my debit card and score two bags of smack.

I've changed dealer to one who will come round my house and drop it off instead of me walking across town to get it off my previous supplier. The old one always asked if he could deal from my house but it's too risky with the police, and Steve my boyfriend goes mad as he doesn't want anything to do with drugs and I am more bothered about upsetting him than worrying about the police coming.

When my previous dealer was homeless I let him come and move in with me. On Christmas Eve last year the police raided my house looking for stolen property and drugs. There was six of them and it took them two hours to go through all of my possessions, they didn't find anything but they carried on visiting me every day for about two months. There was always a difficult copper with one of their side kicks asking me questions about who was dealing what, and where could they find them. I didn't tell them anything, I was scared but more frightened of being knee-capped by a ferocious dealer than of the police.

I am now on first names with the police and they classify me as a vulnerable adult, you can say that again, like I said before, any company is better than the crippling depression of loneliness and solitude.

Been shopping, had to get semi dressed putting long cardigan and jeans on over my night-shirt, brushed my greasy grey hair and shoved on my furry boots that look like slippers. Bought coffee and disposable lighters and got Steve a bottle of wine as he has no money whatsoever. I'm living on my overdraft and get no money until a week on Tuesday, eight days to go without enough money to feed us properly, but enough to pay for Steve's alcoholism and my drug habit. You can always scrape enough money together for these things.

Chapter 16

CORNER SHOP

I met Steve two years ago down at the local pub through a mutual friend. Besides my daughter, Steve is the best thing to happen to me, we are complete opposites. Despite his alcoholism he is solid as a rock, totally dependable, loyal and honest.

I beat about the bush, embarrassed and loud. I am sure that Ramish, the corner shop owner, knows I'm on drugs, besides getting essentials from there I always get twenty pounds cash back. They are Hindus and don't drink alcohol let alone take drugs, he must know that I want the money for narcotics, what else would I want cash back for. They don't like me although I must be one of their best customers. They look at me with so much distaste and they struggle to be polite. They must make a fortune, everything they sell is near enough double than that of the supermarket, convenience shopping costs a lot yet I am too lazy to go to the shops let alone the fact that I look such a mess.

This will be typed by the time you read it, but if you could see my writing on my original you would be able to tell that I struggle to keep my mind focused.

Chapter 17

SOMETHING WRONG

It must have been apparent to those around me when I was growing up that something was wrong. The older generation of the village population used to ask me if everything was all right, I would get a lump in my throat, go bright red and sweaty and mumble that I was all right. I was always fighting back the tears, they must have known that something was wrong, but I was saying nothing, I didn't know what was wrong.

When I was thirteen my parents were called into school and told that I needed to see a child psychologist, my parents refused and came home fuming with me. I got such a good hiding and they said whatever I was doing to make the teachers think I was mad, I was to stop doing. I didn't know what I was doing wrong so I didn't know how to stop. I was always falling to sleep in lessons.

I would tell my parents that I was tired and going to bed, after about quarter of an hour I would put my teddy bears in my bed to make it look like I was asleep and climb out of my bedroom window. If I wasn't down the locks on my boyfriend's boat I would wander around the village, along the tow path in the pitch black and scare myself senseless.

I find it hard to get to sleep, I'm given loads of tablets to help but I just lie in bed awake, my mind turning over and over until I drop off. My dreams are always really vivid yet once I have been awake for ten minutes I have forgotten them. I lie in bed half-awake until lunchtime then I get up and have strong coffee and chain-smoke. If I have any heroin from the night before I smoke that as well.

Before Steve slept with me and had to get up for work, I would stay up all night thinking, thinking is what I'm good at, I can sit still and think for hours. I find myself going over my life to see what would be different if I wasn't ill… *I would work fulltime, probably in sales, I would have a car and my daughter would have stayed living with me.* It's fallen apart from the way in which my life has turned out.

At first I was relieved when I was diagnosed, it made sense to me, I had always wondered about the strange things I had done, wondered why I was so full of energy then plummet into lying in bed 24/7.

When I'm high I think I'm capable of saving everyone. I am renowned in my hometown not just for the walk down the street naked, for taking in the homeless and trying to sort out their drug and drink issues.

Chapter 18

MASTER'S DEGREE

In 2005 I took my masters degree in Reiki healing (Japanese healing art of laying on hands) I thought the whole time I was studying I would set myself up with my own business and heal people for a living. That didn't happen because the rent on the room was astronomical and I would need to work sixty hours a week and be busy from day one.

There was not time for building up a business and if I'm honest I wanted to treat the people who really needed it, the emotionally scarred, drug and alcohol abusers, the bereaved. I knew people that had no money for private treatments they hadn't even heard of Reiki when I talked to them about it.

I take in all sorts of waifs and strays, they stay with me until they have ripped me off and I find out about it. At one point I had four such like people staying with me, Steve was going mad and at one insane point I suggested it to Steve that we move out of the house and into the shed, instead I made them move into the shed. Two of them found somewhere to live and the other two moved into my shed for a few weeks.

Drug addicts are surplus to requirements, no one wants them, they are the unseen dregs of society and their drugs turn them into social pathological liars, they will do anything to get their fix.

Chapter 19

BODY DEALING

A male friend of mine who I met in hospital was raped by a guy who offered my friend a lift home, he lived about five miles out of town. He never had the bloke done for it and duly moved on from smoking a bit of weed and taking the odd acid pill to a full blown heroin addict.

To pay for his addiction he started renting out his arse to anyone who wanted it. He was tiny, had no confidence in himself and had more men up him than he can remember. It never ceases to amaze me just how many men want to have sex with a member of the same sex as they. Anyway (Sam we will call him) was diagnosed with schizophrenia and went from one council flat to another, away from Harborough because he grassed up his friend for dealing dope and if anyone saw him he would get a beating like no tomorrow. He is terrified and I have washed my hands of him as he constantly steals from me and bullies me. He just wants to die and keeps taking overdoses only to wake up eight or nine hours later. He is banned from the ward, across his paperwork in bright red ink it says 'under no circumstances is this patient to be admitted on to the ward, it is not conducive to his treatment.'

Sam used the hospital for somewhere safe to be as he was paranoid and scared of being alone in his flat. The main reason he wasn't allowed back on to the ward is that he treated it as a hotel and was pushing class A drugs on to other patients who were already messed up.

Sam has no conscience whatsoever, he is angry and bitter and after he smacked his mother round the head with a lump of wood he is no longer welcome there either, he is no longer welcome anywhere. He now lives alone, a lonely life with a mind so warped and twisted, no one would be surprised if he went on a killing spree.

The trouble with schizophrenics is they are unpredictable. When they are under the control of medication they are like zombies so they stop taking the tablets and their minds whiz out of control, they are more frightened of others than they are of themselves.

I have tried my hardest to help others less fortunate than myself. Over the passage of time lost souls have turned up at my door for help, I feed them, buy their beers, put a roof over their head when no else would help. I have learned through bitter experience that you can not help those who won't help themselves.

Most of them like their illnesses. It excuses them from society's rules and gives them the time to indulge in their habits. Out of every ten years of being a drug addict seven of those years are spent raising the money, waiting for the dealer to deliver, or going through cold turkey. Is it worth it, far better to be clean and pass the time constructively, walking or looking in a charity shop or something, anything.

Chapter 20

A CANVAS PORTRAIT

I go on courses and paint. I have been on crystal therapy courses, Indian head massage, reflexology, anatomy, physiology and Reiki. All the time I was studying I was deluding myself that I would go back to work in one of those discipline's, I haven't.

I have given away over fifty canvasses I have painted, the pleasure I get from people saying that they are really good and then hanging them on their walls is enough reward. My boyfriend Steve, his mother's house looks like an artist's studio with all my paintings on her walls. I haven't painted for the last five months, Steve keeps trying to get me back into it but it's one of those things that needs inspiration and free flowing ideas. My mind is blank, I'm just not in the mood to paint.

I am in the mood to write. I need to start getting this in order of chapters to make it easier for you to read, *(this will have been sorted out by the time you are reading it)*

I just keep jumping from one idea to the next and not following my decent instinct from smoking fags to chasing the dragon.

To look at me when I am showered and clean, hair

done, make up on and dressed respectably you would never guess what goes on in my 'real' life. Hiding behind a modest looking forty three year old I can fool the best of people, until I open my mouth and blabber on a load of diatribe, skipping from one conversation to random speeches.

I don't care anymore, I'm no longer trying to impress people and join main stream society, it's too much like hard work.

Chapter 21

CHRISTMAS LUNCH AT THE WHITE HORSE

Nearly all of my friends have some sort of mental illness or drug issues. The few of my friends who are sane are broad minded and accept me for who I am, they think I'm funny, I will never grasp why I'm funny I just am. I like making people laugh even if it is at my expense.

All anyone wants is to be happy, but they put it off saying things like 'I'll be happy when such and such has happened,' why wait, why not just be happy where you're at, tomorrow never comes and all that.

People think mistakenly they would be happy if they had more money, a better house, a bigger car, money doesn't make you happy, it just takes some of the stress out of your life. I know that the more money I have the more drugs I would take. For a junkie I am quite disciplined, I pay all my bills and debts off first then what's left over is for drugs.

I need to straighten out; the trouble is I get a buzz from being bad – adrenaline rush. I am sure that I am more addicted to my own brain chemicals than anything else I could put in, maybe my bad habits cause me to produce more adrenaline to send me on a high. Maybe it's just boredom and I need something to do to stimulate myself instead of dossing about in my dressing gown all day.

At least writing this is giving me something to do. At the end of each day I get Julie and Steve to read what I've written and they give me the thumbs up, 'try and write in chapters' is the only criticism I get. *(As I said earlier, by the time you read this it will be in chapters)*

I started smoking dope on my nineteenth birthday, a late starter by all accounts. I was having a birthday party at my house, I had bought my first house when I was nineteen with a bit of help from my dad. My cousin and two other people had locked themselves in the downstairs bathroom, I knew they were up to something by the hushed giggling that was coming out of there. I insisted on being in on the fun so I joined them and locked the door behind me, I took a few nervous drags on the joint and unfortunately started giggling. When I came out of the bathroom my boyfriend demanded to know what we were doing, I told him and he went ape shit and started telling me horror stories of friends of his who jumped off buildings or had ended up in the funny farm. I ignored him and let him stamp off down the street, I had found something that made me giggle and give me the munchies. My sister tried it and threw a 'whitey' going white, shaking and sweating and then threw up in my front garden that was the last time she tried drugs. In a way that's better being put off drugs from a bad experience, I've never had a bad experience on drugs, after the first time at my party I never tried it again for a year.

The next time I was working for a friend in Horncastle, Waitressing, and a friend of his had some weed, I smoked it at his friends house then fell asleep and didn't wake up properly for two days. I was supposed to be going home, which was two hours drive away but instead spent the weekend on the floor of their sitting room.

Dope either gives me the giggles and munchies (*can't stop eating junk food and chocolate*) or it knocks me out and turns me into a zombie like stupor and makes me very vulnerable. Luckily my friends have always kept me safe from perverted old men wanting to shag me.

I was only in Horncastle for a few months over Christmas, my friend had called me for help as they couldn't get any local people to work for them, when I got there I realised why. Jack was half-English and half-Spanish and his mum had had meningitis, which had left her virtually a cabbage, Jack and his step dad Manuel had decided to look after her themselves. She lay in bed with a commode at the side of it; she needed help to get on and off the commode then she would just lie in bed staring at the ceiling with unseeing eyes. I felt sorry for her, I remember her before she fell ill, she was the brain behind 'The Sun Inn' a picturesque country free house and hotel, when she was struck down in her prime with meningitis. Their business folded and they bought 'The White Horse Restaurant' in Horncastle.

The White Horse restaurant should have been successful but Manuel couldn't cater for the size of the place. We had a huge party coming in for Christmas lunch and the thought that Manuel could get away with serving chips instead of roast potatoes, once one customer complained the rest joined in. The place was in uproar and the police were eventually called, needless to say the customers refused to pay their bills, which made The White Horse bankrupt.

I went back home to my little terraced house in Harborough, never knew what happened to Jack, his mum and Manuel. Jack's mother really needed a nurse with her 24/7 yet they couldn't afford that necessity, not luxury.

Chapter 22

PARENTS GRAND
AND GREAT

I often wonder what the less privileged do with their loved ones when illness strikes. My parents were fortunate enough to pay for care for my mum before she went into a private nursing home. At the time it cost six hundred pounds a week but she needed round the clock care. We had a huge string of live in care workers that just ran up huge phone bills and drank my dad's whiskey.

My mum lived in the nursing home for seven years before she died of pneumonia, being unable to move or speak we never knew if she could hear us or know that we were even there, it was heartbreaking. She always said that she never wanted to go into care that she wanted to die at home. My mum needed to go into care, as much as my dad my sister and I never wanted it to come to that. At least there was just enough money my mum had saved to pay for it.

Whenever I went to visit my mum after signing in the visitor's book, the smell of stale urine and old people made me gag. Most of the other patients in the care home were elderly, my mum was in her early forties. She had a private room with ensuite bathroom and the views from her window were picturesque gardens and open countryside. When she was first in there she could see and at least the view was fantastic. I miss my mum, even after all these years I still miss her. Her life was tragic even before she became ill.

My grandma (my mother's mother) died at fifty-three, she was an alcoholic and drank a crate of brown ale and smoked a 100 woodbine cigarettes a day. All I ever remember her eating was tripe and onions, yuk! My grandma never moved from her chair and was always dressed up, made up with her hair dyed black and styled, she reminded me of the Queen, she wore loads of gold necklaces, rings, bracelets and earrings. They earned their money from being publicans hence my grandma's alcoholism.

My granddad (my mother's dad) had only one leg, he lost the other one in World War Two where he was a Japanese prisoner of war for four years. When he was brought home having been on a boat around Australia, he weighed less than four and a half stone and the nurse carried him into my grandma's house. He had been missing presumed dead for four years and my grandma's life had moved on.

My grandparents (my mother's parents) were married before my granddad was subscribed to go to war, he was nineteen. There was no social security back then and my grandma got pregnant with my mum soon after my granddads subscription to go. Back then she was considered an 'old mum' as most women back then started their families in their late teens, my grandma was twenty three.

My mum spent the first five years of her life living with her grandparents (my great grandparents.) Although none of them were diagnosed with manic depression my great grandma, grandma and mother were all depressives with mad mood swings. Back in those days the stigma was much worse than it is today and your loved ones were taken to stately homes in the country never to be seen or heard of again. People didn't talk about it, it brought shame on the family and even back then it was known to be hereditary. My great grandma just lay in bed the whole day bossing everyone else about and my mum spent the first five years of her life living with them. When my two aunties came along mum went back to her parents to help with her two younger sisters (my aunties.)

My grandma (my mum's mother) was always drunk but never happy, they lived in an immaculate bungalow that my grandfather took care of with military role. My mother was caned daily by my grandfather and they were strict beyond belief. My mum met my dad in the pub my grandparents ran and deliberately got pregnant when she was seventeen. She had had enough of being chamber maiden, working behind the bar and holding down a full time job at the accountants. My mum was very clever, and a brilliant musician playing the piano for the pleasure of all. My mum was thrown out by her parents for getting pregnant and went to live in the overcrowded house with my dad, his four surviving siblings and his parents (my grandparents on my father's side.) They had a shotgun wedding at the registry office when my mum was eighteen and my dad twenty-four.

Times were hard for my mum and dad, my mum's parents gave them fifty pounds deposit for their first house, my dad earned thirteen pounds a week and dug graves to make ends meet. Then when my sister was four months old my mum fell pregnant with me, at the time my sister had diphtheria and they didn't know if she would survive, the last thing they needed was another hungry child to feed. My mum would go and work the twilight shift in a factory and my dad worked away most of the time fitting industrial batteries all over the country…

Whilst my mum was at work she would leave my sister and I in a lobster pot playpen whilst she went off to work. It wasn't until my dad's sister (my aunt on my father's side) called round on the off chance that it was found out that my mum was leaving us unattended for four hours. Anything could have happened, my mum had no idea how to look after us whatsoever.

As children we were frequently smacked, our knickers pulled down and hit across our bottoms with a leather slipper. After bath time on a Sunday evening my mum would smack both of us like this for all the things we had done wrong through the week that she hadn't found out about, she thought it was little punishment. It was, compared to the beatings she had daily with my granddads walking cane.

My maternal grandparents never thought that my dad was good enough for their daughter. My dad came from a big family, there were six children one of whom died when she was eighteen of some mysterious illness. They all lived in a council house that was tidy but filthy. When we went to eat at their house there was always silver fish in with the boiled veg, granddad used to say it was free protein. They kept chickens and geese and grew all of their vegetables in the massive garden. My dad bred rabbits so there was very little shopping to be done, everything we ate came from these sources.

During the time we lived in Harborough there was a fizzy pop delivery lorry and my favourite treat was Dandelion and Burdock. There was a lorry that also delivered coal and my granddad George used to drive this lorry delivering coal for all the open fires that ran the back boilers for heating. We got really excited when it was the day for pop and coal deliveries. My granddad George didn't have to go to war because his job was one of those exempt as they were seen as necessities. He always had sweets for the children, boiled mint ones that we all gathered round the lorry for. Due to his job he was extremely strong and could pick both my sister and I up, one in each arm and twiddle us round until we were giddy, then he would put us down and laugh as we wobbled off back up the street.

Chapter 23

FUNKY MONKEY TALES

There were loads of kids living on our street…

My best friend Vicky was the youngest of six children, whose father had died before she was born, I loved being round her house. Vicky's mum was the 'nit nurse' at our school, the district nurse, all of her children were 'self-raising' as she worked all hours God sent to provide for them, she was lovely.

I liked it best round Vicky's house when her mother was at work, we could bounce on the bed pretending we were Olga Corbett *(the Russian gymnast who was tiny.)* Vicky was great fun and I wanted to go and live with them, just round the corner from our house. I was so frightened of the dark and was glad for the street light directly outside my window so it was never completely black in my own bedroom. In the winter when it was dark, I would hide behind Vicky's neighbour's fence and peep out to make sure no one was coming then make a dash for Vicky's front door.

Round Vicky's house was always good fun, she had two older brothers and three older sisters. The boy's never bothered with us, staying in their room but her sisters used to play and they had a dog called Benji, I always wanted dog when I was growing up but we weren't allowed pets. We had our own gang called 'the funky monkeys' and our head office was their conservatory.

One day we decided to break into the old chip shop that had been shut down for hygienic reasons, not surprisingly, there was dried on grease everywhere and a dead rat in one of the filthy fridge's. The people that ran the TV repair shop over the road threatened to call the police, they didn't but my sister has such a guilty conscience that one evening she confessed to our parents. She was praised for confessing and I got a good hiding, I was already in bed and was woken by dad's hard hand on my bottom, fancy not waking me up first and then smacking me. From that day onwards I was scared to go to sleep in my high rise bed.

I had the box room and because it was so small I had three chests of drawers in a row with a mattress on top for my bed, at the end of my bed there was just enough room for my books. Sometimes I would be deliberately naughty so I was smacked and sent to my room, I would rather be in my bedroom reading Enid Blyton's story books than sitting downstairs watching telly with my mum, dad and sister.

I loved reading and could lose myself in Enid Blyton's stories of boarding schools and magical tales of made up animals. I wanted to go to boarding school, she made it sound so exciting, anything to be away from my family sounded good.

Chapter 24

BLOW JOB BOB

In my chequered past I had a boyfriend who went to boarding school from the age of six. He told me stories about teachers that would accuse one of the boys in the class of farting. Then he would line all the boys in the class against the wall and sniff their bottoms, accuse one of them of doing the dirty deed and have them sent to his office later in the day to have their shorts and pants pulled down, made to bend over the desk and be caned. This was the least of the abuse those vulnerable children received with no parents to protect them. My boyfriend used to run away all the time to his mothers who lived only ten miles from the school, he was always taken back.

Both his parents had re married and no one wanted him. Regular working class people always look at the privileged middle classes of having better childhood's, the truth is money doesn't buy their kids happiness. Boarding school was a dumping ground the rich parents used so they didn't have the commitments family life brings. The truth about middle English families makes what happens to the working class pale into insignificance. At least we were protected from paedophilic teachers and warped matrons, the only physical abuse we got were smacks, nothing compared to the mind bending sexual abuse those boys suffered.

From the age of six this boyfriend never went back to live with either of his parents, he has two stepbrothers on his father's side, his mother couldn't have any more children. We split up after three years as he had a blow job from the local village gay. He let me believe it was my paranoia that people gave us funny looks and stared at me, everyone knew in the village except me, we were the laughing stock and when he finally admitted to me about the blow job I left and since referred to him as blow job Bob. I left everything I owned there, patted the dog goodbye, picked up my keys and handbag and drove the fifty miles back home to Harborough. I was gutted and felt dirty to think of him being sucked off by the old drunkard in the local dive of a pub, he had no idea about village life.

I was brought up in a village and gossip is spread quicker than warm butter on bread. I was so ashamed and angry that he was using my illness and saying I was paranoid whilst all the time the whole village knew. I was so glad that I hadn't sold my house in Harborough and I wasn't stuck with him or homeless. It took me years to trust someone again and I spent the next eight years single, the majority of this time I spent in bed or curled on the floor in my sitting room with my dressing gown on. I chain smoked dope one after the other an ounce and a half a week, I was spending ninety pounds a week on the stuff, not leaving enough money to eat or pay the bills. I had no gas or electric and would sit in the dark except for a candle. I smoked dope morning, noon and night, if I had visitors it didn't matter who they were, I just wanted them to go so I could carry on smoking, I was numb.

Support workers would come round and gauge how close to suicide I was and I was duly taken in and out of the ward, at the time I preferred being in hospital. I did little at home but even less when I was in hospital.

The only company I like are people who have similar or the same illness, I feel more at home with a room full of schizophrenics than normal people. I don't feel like a second class citizen with them, we all understand each other.

Chapter 25

A DANGEROUS PLACE

There are many interesting people in hospital…

At one point a guy called Arthur was in, he was an alcoholic and taken up injecting himself in the groin with whisky, his mouth was green with infection, his lips cracked and dried out, he was in hospital for a detox and shook violently the whole time. I got on really well with him, he was about forty five yet looked a hundred, it's amazing what damage people can do to themselves with alcohol, it should be illegal just as much as heroin is. His wife had left him and took the kids when he was slipping into his habit, he went from drinking strong lager to injecting whisky in the space of less than a year. After his wife had left he had nothing to hold him stable and found himself unemployed, unemployable and homeless.

These people stay in hospital until a council flat is found for them. At one point in the distant past Arthur would have been a good looking, tall dude the remnants of those good looks were just visible. I felt sorry for his wife, she wasn't expecting her good catch to wither away to a stooping, slumped shadow of his former self.

I also made good friends with a guy called Terry, we lived in the same town, when he lived at Gartree and I lived at Foxton we went to school together. His mum dropped dead in front of him when he was four years old, his dad re married and his new wife was awful to Terry. He left him when he was sixteen to live with a gay guy who was forcing himself on him. After joining the Army, Terry lived in Germany where he got married and had two children. His job in the Army was to carry out post mortems chopping up his colleagues to find out what had caused their death. Terry would come round to my house and if I gave him any dope to smoke he would eat it. He once drank a bottle of nitrates (poppers) that gay guys sniff just before they reach orgasm, I used to sniff it, it makes your heart beat so fast, gives you a massive head rush and makes you sweat like a pig. Terry also used to drink a whole jar of coffee and any alcohol in the house. Terry hated being in his council flat and would often stay on the sofa so he didn't have to go home. At one point Terry was holding down a job translating his fluent German into English. He was called into the hospital, as he was not adhering to his medication, Doctor Beaton sectioned him and really wound him up, she was more like a prison governor than a psychiatrist and had no compassion for her patients.

Terry went into the smoke room on the ward, the only other person was a new female patient, he asked her for a cigarette and she refused him. He beat her up so badly that she had to have her scalp shaven and glued back together, none of the staff on the ward at the time went to her assistance. They called C & R *(control and restraint)* and it took them five minutes to get there, he has near enough killed her by then. Terry is now in a high security mental prison at Her Majesty's pleasure, he will never be out and by now will have given up, he is totally institutionalised, it's such a shame when the staff wind up the patients to such an extent that they flip. This would never have happened if Doctor Beaton had done her job properly. Terry was usually very amiable and friendly, he was done for attempted murder all over a single cigarette.

You are supposed to be safe in hospital and that young girl was offered no protection. She was already mentally ill to be there in the first place, following that incident she will never recover, never feel safe anywhere.

Chapter 26

A WALK TO AMERICA

It was a wet Wednesday afternoon that I went to outpatients to visit my Chinese psychiatrist for our weekly meeting. I was talking rapidly and changing the subject at random. It was obvious to her that I was way too high and she suggested a rest on the ward. I begged her not to make me go as I was seeing my daughter later and had a friend's birthday party to go to. She said in her Chinese accent, 'You too high, you too high, take some lorazepan you like lorazepan,' she said she would send an ambulance to collect me in the morning. Big mistake on her part, I had got it into my head that the hospital was trying to poison me with tablets and I had no intention of either taking the tablets or going to hospital the next morning.

I went to visit my daughter and was talking a lot of crap about Henry Kissinger being the anti Christ and I was going on a mission from God. We went over to my dad's but no one was in so I left a garbled note, which my daughter copied and I told her off for not thinking what to write herself. She was only six bless her, and copying my note wasn't really a problem I was just snappy, I dropped her off at her nana's and went home to prepare for the party.

I was driving so took some fruit juice to drink instead of wine, I was as high as a kite and dominated the party with my never ending diatribe, looking back with sane eyes I can see what a pain in the butt I was. I told the host if I was never seen again it was because the hospital had diagnosed me and the evidence was in the bathroom bin where I had put the prescription for lorazepan.

Because I drove a big Mercedes Benz my dad had given me, I decided I would walk to the M6 where I had met a broken down traveller who stayed at a farm nearby. I had picked him up on the side of the road whilst on my way to Birmingham one night. I am always playing the role of Good Samaritan, I believe I'm doing God's work, not that he needs my help. I got changed into a pair of jeans that my friend had given me, they were two sizes too big and an old black T-shirt and four-inch high black witches boots. I set off from home in the dark with a pack of ten Benson and Hedges cigarettes and a box of matches. In my fuddled mind I thought I would be able to get to the farm before daylight.

I was paranoid about being seen that every time I saw the headlights of a car I would throw myself down on the pavement. At one point as I was lying on the pavement facing the night sky and watching the stars, I saw a shooting star and was convinced it was God watching me. Because I didn't want to be seen I decided to go across country and started walking through the fields. It was pitch black with no street lamps to see by, I stumbled along in my ridiculous boots, talk about inappropriate clothing, I had no coat and even though it was summer it was freezing cold at night in just a T-shirt. When I was in a field of sheep they would all start following me bleating so loudly in the silence, I would keep stopping to shoo them away but they kept following me. In the end I climbed over the hedge into the next field. I was stung by stinging nettles and scratched to pieces all over my bare arms, I carried on going on my mission, which I believe God had sent me on.

I thought I could tell this traveller that Henry Kissinger was the anti Christ and that he would somehow get me to America to shoot him, I hadn't taken my passport but that seemed a minor detail. All night I walked through the fields not thinking I might disturb a bull, I didn't, but it hadn't occurred to me at the time. I was having my period at the time and wasn't using any sanitary protection so my blue jeans were covered in blood, I must have looked a right sight!

When daylight broke I found a disused trailer in a field and decided to sleep for a while, I was convinced that the world was spinning in the opposite direction. No one could see me from the road but when the odd car went by on the country lane I thought they were all going backwards. It's amazing the tricks your mind plays on you when you are not taking tablets to hold you in a precarious sanity.

I carried on, sleeping by day in the warm sunshine and walking all night. I had completely miscalculated just how long this walk was and how long it would take me. I walked along the edge of the motorway and when I needed a wee I would drop my jeans and pee on the motorway embankment, cars were racing by and not to my knowledge at the time, the police were called. I was on the front page of the Leicester Mercury although I never found this out until after my expedition.

I eventually reached the farm after stopping at a quarry works. The man on the reception point took me in and gave me a very welcome mug of steaming hot tea and gave me his pack up of cheese sandwiches and crisps and a bar of chocolate. It was the first food and hot drink I had had in three days.

When I was passing through a village on my travels, there was a house for sale with an outside tap. I stopped to have a drink from this tap and water never tasted so good, it was the first drink I had had in over two days. I was parched, filthy and stood out like a sore thumb, the few people I saw all stared at me like I was a vision from a hell. The house next door to the house for sale had a mad, barking dog and the owner was encouraging the dog to bark saying, 'go on boy, what's there?' They cut my drink short, I could have stayed there drinking from the tap forever it was so welcome.

Because of all the energy I had used and had little

food, the jeans I was wearing kept slipping down and I had no belt so I was having to hold them up with one hand. My boots had worn all the way through and I had massive blisters on the soles of my feet, I was in agony and was delirious, not just from my mental health problems but the treacherous journey I had undertaken. I carried on in my confused state of mind until I reached the farm that the traveller stayed at. I knocked on the side house door, to my horror someone other than Kieran answered, I asked where he was and they had never heard of him. I broke into one of the sheds and peed in a barrel full of bird feathers.

When the farmer opened the door I was asleep on an old thrown out sofa in the barn, he was fuming, the typical red-faced angry farmer. He asked what I was doing there and I explained that I was looking for Kieran because I needed his help to get to America to shoot the anti Christ Henry Kissinger. He took me into the farmhouse and his rotund wife rang a number on the phone to contact Kieran. I garbled on to Kieran that I was the woman who stopped on the motorway to help him when he had broken down, he was in Ireland harvesting at another farm, as it was the end of the summer. He said if I could survive for a week he would come and fetch me, no one could survive a week the state I was in. After having a glass of water with the farmer's wife I went on my way, I stopped on the opposite side of the farm and crawled into a ditch.

Not to my knowledge at the time, my dad had

turned up at the farm and had missed me by minutes, they were searching for me and I didn't even know that anyone knew I was missing. My boyfriend at the time lived in Birmingham and they thought I was on my way walking to his house. They originally knew nothing about my friendship with Kieran, the man at the quarry told them the directions to the farm, he had given me his fluorescent jacket, which I had discarded because it was too bright. My dad had to go and identify a body they thought was me. Obviously it wasn't me but it must have been really traumatic for him to have travelled the half hour journey to the hospital to look at the body of a different young woman.

During the trek back home I went through an oil seed rape field, when you drive through the country this looks like a field full of bright yellow flowers. In fact it is thick, dense and prickly, not the fluffy stuff it looks like, I had picked up a long branch, which I was using as a walking stick. I used it to chop my way through the oil seed rape, it must have taken me over an hour to smash my way through on the scorching hot, summer afternoon. I thought I would die in the field. Something strong inside of me kept me going, when I finally got to the other side I had to wade through some stagnant puddles where someone had been fly tipping.

After this I started hitch hiking to wherever the driver wanted to take me, when you are high you have absolutely no common sense and no fear, no way of recognising danger. The second car, which drove by picked me up, he was living in his car, as his job as a long distance lorry driver was based miles away from his house, which he rented out. He had tea-making facilities in his car, a gas burner and a tin kettle, a flask of milk and a carton of tea bags. I must have drank ten cups in just as many minutes.

He told me about his schizophrenic mother who every so often would pack suitcases and take him and his sister on a walk about, she had committed suicide three years earlier and he really missed her. He felt the same way as I do about hospital admission and treatment, the staff on wards simply don't care or don't have the time to care. He was on his way to work and was taking his cargo to Germany, I contemplated cutting off my long curly hair and hiding in his truck and going to Germany like a refugee but he talked me out of it, it was a stupid idea in the first place. He drove me to Lutterworth and dropped me off with all the small change he had and a thin summer jacket, wishing me luck he drove off.

I climbed up on to a disused railway and went to sleep until the cold woke me up. I walked back into the town centre and the next lift I got was from a cleaner who had just finished work in the Bank. It was around 6.30 a.m. and she asked me where I was going, I said wherever you are, I was stark staring crazy and she was sympathetic and kind. She was going back home to Leicester so I hopped into the passenger seat and off we went.

When we got there she dropped me off in a car park that had a block of toilets, they were filthy with graffiti all over the walls. I thought they were messages from God and spent the rest of the morning reading all the scratched in messages, they didn't make any sense at all to me and I felt I was letting God down because I couldn't decipher the scribbled writings. I sat on one of the dirty toilet seats and went to sleep.

When I woke up I went to a small café and had enough money to buy a cup of tea, I warmed my freezing hands around the mug. People were staring at me and gesticulating, I didn't know it at the time but I was on the front page of their local paper and they must have recognised me. I quickly drank my tea and then trotted off down the crowded street.

I got my next lift off three lads who were off to Billing aquadrome, they dropped me off in Husbands Bosworth and I hid in a closed down pub. I really needed to go to the toilet so I had a poo behind a tree in the overgrown garden. I waited for hours for the boys to come back for me, they never did, so I thought I would walk the eight miles back to Market Harborough but I knew my feet wouldn't have made it.

I went into the local store and bought a banana and saw the paper for the first time, there I was in black and white photographed looking barking mad, I started panicking and left the shop sharpish. One of the local builders was in the shop and he took me back to his house once he had bought the paper, he and his three mates were drinking strong lager and smoking dope. There was a tacky porn tape playing on the TV, they offered me a beer, and I said I would rather have a cup of tea but I didn't refuse the dope, I was gagging for a fag as I had run out of Benson & Hedges two days before. I choked away on the joint whilst telling them what I was doing, they were all laughing at the dishevelled mad woman who was front page news, they were bothered about the police turning up but let me stay over on their sofa.

It was early evening when some friends of theirs called round, they exclaimed, 'it's a girl' obviously they rarely had female company. One of the friends was going into Harborough in the morning and we arranged for him to pick me up the next day. I slept like a baby on that sofa in the warmth with my feet out of my battered boots; I was nearly home after my mission. In the morning the man friend came and dropped me off back at my house. I had left my front and back doors open and found them both locked. My boyfriend from Birmingham had been and had joined my dad and the police in the search for me. By chance he had come round to my house to see if everything was okay and had seen my long black hair going through my gate into my back garden, he let me in and gave me a fag.

He went along with my crazy idea to go to Billing aquadrome in Northampton. I walked down to the Recreation Park at the end of my street and walked along the disused rail track where he picked me up in his van with the dog inside. The dog was going loopy to see me and off we went to Billing aquadrome, all the time I was ranting on about my mission whilst he listened incredulously. When we got near to Billing we stopped at a Little Chef and I rang my dad's house, my sister answered and was really angry with me saying that my dad and June (my dad's girlfriend) were out looking for me. I told her to call off the police and that I was safe, she said she would tell the police that I had called and they would be on their way to collect me, she fumed about all the trouble and worry I had caused. I got back in the van with our mad dog and my boyfriend drove us back to his house.

I went for a bath, well overdue by the smell of me, and weighed myself on the bathroom scales and had lost over one and a half stone in six days. I was starving but my stomach had shrunk, so I just nibbled on a bit of salad. I needed something more substantial but my boyfriend hadn't been shopping since I was missing and there was nothing else in the house to eat but dog food, I didn't fancy that so I just drank mug after mug of sweet tea.

My boyfriend's best friend was the sergeant at a police station in Birmingham so we were asking him the best thing for me to do. We had contacted the police and told them I was safe, they wanted me to go to the local police station to be identified but Doug my boyfriend's friend said, make them come to the house otherwise they would take me straight back to hospital and that was the last place I wanted to be. Within the hour the police (two of them) came to the house to question my boyfriend and me. I was wearing a pair of his jogging bottoms and a sweatshirt that were absolutely massive on me.

The police really wanted to take me then and asked loads of questions about where I had been. I turned into the best liar ever and said that I had walked all the way to Birmingham, I said nothing about the lifts I had had and that I was picked up by my boyfriend at my house. I am such a bad liar they knew I wasn't telling the truth but there was nothing they could do.

I spent the next five months locked up in my boyfriend's house, not taking my medication, he kept me locked in because my behaviour was so unpredictable and I felt safer with the world locked out of his house with me inside. I ran up a huge phone bill calling all my friends excitedly about my mission and that I was sure my travelling friend would sort out Henry Kissinger.

By the end of my five months incarceration without my medication I was totally insane. My boyfriend had had enough and took me back to hospital in Leicester where I was sectioned for six months under the mental health act. I was so angry and hurt and felt that I had been betrayed. By the time my section was lifted I didn't want to go home to my seemingly massive terraced house, I had become totally institutionalised.

All you have to do in hospital is make tea and change your bed sheets once a week and I wasn't looking forward to having to run a house again.

Chapter 27

SMOKE ROOM

During my stay in hospital I had made loads of friends whilst sitting in the smoke room. The smoke room is like sitting at a railway station waiting for a train that never comes. It is only in the smoke room that any counselling happens between patients, I would sit in there for hour's chain smoking and listening to other patient's life histories.

I was officially adopted by my good friend Anne who didn't have a daughter and I didn't have a mum. Anne has the same disorder as me and we often sat up all night talking about the different episodes of our lives. Over the course of our ten year friendship she has done the funniest things, she often leaves the house in her pyjamas with her coat over her and drive off on her missions. She also has a strong faith the same as me and is convinced God is watching over her 24/7.

Anne once drove to East Midlands airport with her coat over her nightdress and just her purse, no luggage or handbag, the pockets of her coat were full and she was ready to board a plane. She was convinced her boyfriend was trying to kill her, her boyfriend called the hospital and all the airports were put on lookout for her. She was picked up by the police and much to her dismay was taken to hospital. What a sight, Anne is no spring chicken and is a good four stone overweight and half her teeth are missing. Before she left her husband she was quite well to do, she speaks in a posh accent and carries herself well, yet she is practically always inappropriately dressed as in a 'much younger woman's style.'

There was a knock on my door early one morning and my boyfriend Steve answered it, he had not met Anne before and was surprised to see her in her nightie and coat at my front door. I got up to see what was going on and introduced Steve to Anne. Anne was complaining about having chapped lips and the only cream I had in the house was Anusol (haemorrhoid cream) which I gave her. She promptly spread piled cream all over her face so she had a shiny white face a bit like a clown halfway through makeup. After this she went home again, she wasn't very well and really needed to have the support team round, I rang them as we have the same group covering us, they went out to see her and she called me a grass and was not pleased.

You never know what to do for the best in these situations, it was obvious Anne needed help but she didn't like the help offered to her.

When we are high we are terrified of being taken to hospital; it is a dreadful place to be when you are high and full of energy. There is nothing to do but pace about from the day room to the smoke room (now being changed to activity room) as smoking isn't allowed on the ward. This has caused chaos as most of the patient's smoke, limiting them to the privilege of leaving the ward for a set smoke break is torture for the patients.

There are times at night when a patient kicks off because they want a fag and chewing nicotine gum just doesn't cure it. I have seen a big male patient totally lose it with the staff throwing files and paperwork everywhere, attacking a member of staff purely for the want of a fag.

Chapter 28

SAFETY SUITE

I have been in the safety suite (padded cell, as it was once known) twice in my fifteen-year history of being on and off the ward it is really degrading. The first time I was in was Christmas 1998.

The first Christmas I had spent without my daughter I had been going screwy all day at my dad's house where my sister and her three daughters were staying. I made a Christmas card that was insane to say the least. My youngest niece had won Athlete of the Year and had a cup on the kitchen table with 'winner' on it. I thought it was a posh ashtray and was flicking ash in it much to my sister's annoyance, I was under the impression that I had left my body and was letting my mum use it to be back at home for Christmas. I was behaving how my mother would have reacted if she had seen the mess her immaculate home had descended into. My sister and I were arguing, she couldn't tell that I was being mum and she rang my dad to come home from his girlfriends, as I was too much for her to handle. As soon as my dad got home he slapped me across my bottom and said, behave yourself.

I had been running up and down the street in a bloody g-string and nothing else when Doctor Fox arrived, she advised to take me to hospital much against my wishes. My dad gave me his dressing gown to put on, which I screwed up in a ball and hugged like a teddy bear.

So off we all went to hospital, my dad, his girlfriend and my sister, with me in my soiled knickers hugging a dressing gown. I was ranting on in my mad way until we reached the hospital, I refused to get out of the car and my dad coaxed me out. The staff accompanied me to the ward and my family left to carry on with what was left of Christmas Day, no one got Christmas dinner that day.

I was carried through the ward by a team of five control and restraint much to my annoyance and was struggling against them the whole time. They took me into a side room where I started to rip up pamphlets and was talking like a baby. Doctor Beeston was called and I was pinned down by four nurses and was injected with a strong sedative, they then dragged me face down and naked apart from the bloody knickers into the 'safety suite,' I was locked in for over six hours. I needed to go to the toilet but the nurses wouldn't let me out until control and restraint came, I weed in the corner of the 'safety suite.'

When they let me out I was really groggy and three nurses bathed me, provided me with sanitary towels and was given a pair of lost property knickers to hold the towel in place. I was given a pair of hospital pyjamas, which had green bottoms and a faded orange top, I had to hold the bottoms up as the elastic around them had gone, what a sorry state to get in but I was as high as a kite.

During my time in the 'safety suite' although I was lying on the mattress with a blanket over me, my mind felt as though it had left my body and I was dead. Because of the injection I felt paralysed, but my mind was imagining that I was with my daughter opening presents, I would roll myself up in the blanket then open up the blanket with laughter.

In the dim and distant past on my crusade to try all illegal drugs I snorted ketamin, horse tranquilliser, the trip I was on in the 'safety suite' was like my mind was totally detached from my body and was spinning round so fast with different ideas popping in and out of it. The next day was Boxing Day.